HOW TO START A PUBLISHING COMPANY

Mastering Every Aspect Of Bringing Books To Life

Jeanelle K. Douglas

Copyright © 2024 by Jeanelle K. Douglas. All rights reserved. No part of this book, HOW TO START A PUBLISHING COMPANY, may be reproduced, stored in a retrieval system, or transmitted in any form or by any means, electronic, mechanical, photocopying, recording, or otherwise, without the prior written permission of the author, Jeanelle K. Douglas.

Table of Contents

Introduction 5

    Significance of Publishing Companies 8

    Those This Book Is Useful 16

Market Research And Analysis 18

    Developing a Business Strategy 20

    Legal and financial considerations 23

    Skills And Competencies Needed For The Business 27

    Things To Consider Before Starting a Publishing Company 31

    Business Model Approach in Publishing 38

Setting up of office space 42

    Understanding the State of the Publishing Industry 46

    Challenges in the Publishing Industry 51

The Potential of the Publishing Industry 53

    Content acquisition and management 56

    Acquiring rights and permissions 61

    Managing authors and content producers 65

Importance of Editing and quality control in Publishing 68
Publishing methods and distribution............................... 72
Differences between Print media and Digital Way of Publishing 75
Factors to be considered in each Printing Processes..... 81
Distribution channels and strategy................................ 85
Selling and sales strategy 92
The Significance of Brand Identity............................... 96
Marketing Plan... 98
Online Presence 104
Sales channels and revenue generation...................... 108
Collaboration with writers and influencers................. 112
Conclusion 115

INTRODUCTION

In today's digital age, the publishing industry is undergoing a transformation. Aspiring authors and content creators are seeking new ways to share their stories, expertise, and creativity with the world. In this ever-changing landscape, starting a publishing company offers a unique opportunity to not only contribute to the rich fabric of literature but also carve out a niche in a rapidly expanding industry.

This book is a comprehensive guide for those looking to embark on an entrepreneurial journey in the publishing industry. Whether you're a passionate writer looking to self-publish your work or an aspiring entrepreneur with a vision for a thriving publishing enterprise, this book will equip you with the knowledge, insights, and practical strategies you need to navigate the complexities of starting and running a successful publishing company. Prospective publishers can use this book as a road map, guiding them through every step of the process, from laying the groundwork for their business to establishing a strong presence in the competitive publishing scene.

Through a combination of in-depth research, real-world case studies, and actionable recommendations, readers will gain a comprehensive understanding of the key ideas and practices that drive the success of modern publishing organizations. The process of starting a publishing company is not without its challenges. From understanding the nuances of copyright law to navigating the complexities of distribution channels, prospective publishers must have the knowledge and skills to overcome obstacles and seize opportunities.

"How to Start a Publishing Company" provides readers with the skills and resources they need to overcome these obstacles and become successful publishers. The book covers a wide range of topics, including market research and analysis, business planning, content acquisition and management, publishing procedures and distribution, marketing and sales techniques, and much more.

Each chapter has been thoughtfully prepared to provide readers with concrete insights and practical advice that they can immediately apply to their own publishing projects.

Whether you're a seasoned entrepreneur looking to diversify your company's portfolio or a passionate book lover hoping to make a name for yourself in the publishing world, "How to Start a Publishing Company" is your go-to guide for turning your dreams into reality. Join us on this incredible journey as we build and run a thriving publishing company.

Publishing companies have a significant impact on shaping our cultural environment, encouraging intellectual discourse, and preserving information for future generations. Their significance goes far beyond the simple dissemination of books and other written materials; they act as custodians of our shared heritage and catalysts for social and intellectual progress.

Significance of Publishing Companies

1. Knowledge Preservation and Dissemination: Publishing companies serve as stewards of human knowledge, preserving the ideas, stories, and discoveries of past and present generations. They ensure the long-term preservation of important information by publishing books, journals, and other written materials. From great literary masterpieces to new scientific discoveries, publishing companies facilitate the dissemination of information across geographical and cultural boundaries, improving the lives of readers all over the world.

2. Publishers promote cultural diversity and preserve linguistic heritage: They demonstrate the richness and diversity of human expression by publishing works in multiple languages and from various cultural perspectives. Publishing companies contribute to a more inclusive and integrated global community by publishing translated works, indigenous literature, and multicultural publications that foster cross-cultural understanding and appreciation.

3. Platform of Intellectual Discourse: Publishing companies offer a forum for intellectual debate and idea sharing. They promote meaningful debates on a wide range of topics, including politics, philosophy, science, and the arts, through books, articles, and scholarly journals. Publishing businesses promote human knowledge and society by releasing books that challenge conventional wisdom and spark thought-provoking debates.

4. **Promoting Creativity and Innovation:** Publishing companies play an important role in encouraging creativity and innovation. They promote creativity and intellectual discovery by providing a forum for authors, artists, and researchers to share their ideas with the rest of the world. Publishing companies assist creators in reaching a larger audience and realizing their artistic and intellectual potential by providing editing services, marketing support, and distribution networks.

5. **Economic and employment opportunities:** Publishing companies help the economy by generating revenue, creating jobs, and supporting related industries. Editors, designers, sales agents, and distributors are examples of the

diverse staff that publishing companies employ. They also support the livelihoods of authors, artists, and other creative by providing a means for them to profit from their work.

6. A catalyst for social change: Publishing companies can effect social change and influence public opinion on important social issues. They contribute to social justice and the promotion of a more equitable society by publishing works that challenge dominant social conventions, fight for justice and equality, and elevate marginalized voices. Publishing companies can inspire real societal reforms by writing books that elicit empathy, compassion, and understanding.

7. Accessibility and Education: Publishing companies contribute to the accessibility of knowledge and education by making books and educational materials available to a large audience. Publishing companies ensure that people with diverse learning styles and abilities have access to educational resources in a variety of formats, including print, digital, and audio. This accessibility promotes lifelong learning, enables individuals to pursue academic and professional objectives, and contributes to a more educated and informed society.

8. Cultural Legacy and Historic Preservation: Publishers play an important role in preserving our cultural and historical heritage. Publishing works of literature, history, and memoirs captures the essence of many times, communities, and individuals, allowing future generations to learn about the past. Furthermore, publishing companies help to preserve cultural items and manuscripts through specialized publishing efforts and collaborations with museums, archives, and cultural institutions.

9. Global Connectivity and Exchange: Publishers serve as cultural bridges, facilitating global communication and exchange. They provide readers with diverse perspectives and experiences from all over the world via translated works, multinational partnerships, and cross-border distribution networks. This global exchange of ideas fosters cross-cultural understanding, empathy, and tolerance, resulting in a more interconnected and peaceful global community.

10. Publishing companies innovate technology: Resulting in advancements in digital publishing, printing, and distribution. Investing in cutting-edge technology such as e-books, print-on-demand, and augmented reality improves the reading experience and expands access to literature and educational resources. This invention benefits both readers and authors while also improving the overall sustainability and efficiency of the publishing industry.

11. Community Development and Engagement: Publishing companies help to promote community development and involvement. Book clubs, author events, literary festivals, and online communities allow for meaningful connections, conversations, and collaborations. This sense of community fosters a love of reading, stimulates intellectual curiosity, and connects people interested in books and learning.

12. Environmental sustainability: Publishing companies are placing more emphasis on environmental sustainability and incorporating eco-friendly practices throughout the publishing process. They reduce their environmental impact and help to create a more sustainable publishing ecosystem by using sustainable materials, lowering carbon emissions, and implementing responsible printing and distribution processes. This commitment to sustainability aligns with larger efforts to combat climate change and preserve the natural environment for future generations.

This book's primary goal is to provide prospective entrepreneurs and publishing enthusiasts with a comprehensive guide to starting and running a successful publishing company.

Through extensive analysis, practical insights, and real-world examples, the book aims to provide readers with the knowledge, skills, and tools they need to navigate the complexities of the publishing industry and realize their entrepreneurial goals. One of the book's main goals is to simplify the process of starting a publishing company and show readers a clear path to success.

By breaking down the various steps of the publishing process, from initial concept to operational execution, the book equips readers with the skills and tactics they need to confidently and clearly navigate each step.

Another important goal of the book is to provide a comprehensive understanding of the publishing industry and its dynamics. By covering topics such as market research, business planning, content acquisition, distribution methods, marketing, and sales, the book provides readers with a comprehensive understanding of the major factors that contribute to a publishing company's success.

Readers can make more informed decisions and navigate the competitive publishing landscape by learning about industry trends, best practices, and potential pitfalls.

The book aims to promote creativity and innovation in the publishing industry. The book encourages readers to think creatively and experiment with new ways of creating and distributing information by presenting case studies, success stories, and examples of unique publishing endeavors. Readers can establish a publishing company that not only profits financially but also benefits society and the environment by adhering to ethical principles and employing sustainable methods.

In essence, "How to Start a Publishing Company" seeks to provide aspiring entrepreneurs with the knowledge, skills, and motivation required to establish and run a successful publishing company. The book is a comprehensive guide to the various aspects of publishing entrepreneurship, providing readers with the tools and strategies they need to navigate the industry's complexities, foster innovation, and build a publishing company that thrives in an ever-changing landscape.

Those This Book Is Useful

Individuals from various professions, such as journalism, media production, arts administration, and digital content development, who want to explore new career paths or start their own businesses in the creative sectors are the target audience for the book. These people may come from a variety of backgrounds, including journalism, media production, arts administration, and digital content development. For them, the book offers a unique opportunity to learn about publishing as a viable career or business venture, as well as critical insights into the skills, tools, and techniques required to thrive in the industry.

The book also appeals to anyone interested in social impact and community participation. These individuals may be interested in learning about how publishing companies can promote social transformation, cultural preservation, and community empowerment. For them, the book is a thought-provoking look at how publishing shapes society's narratives, amplifies marginalized perspectives, and encourages discussion of pressing social issues.

The book encourages readers to consider the broader societal implications of their publishing efforts, emphasizing the power of publishing as a weapon for social justice and community development. These individuals may be interested in how digital advancements are transforming the publishing industry, from e-books and audiobooks to online platforms and social media marketing.

It gives readers the information and skills they need to confidently and adaptably navigate the digital publishing age. Whether they are aspiring entrepreneurs, industry professionals, writers, book lovers, freelancers, business enthusiasts, or social change advocates, the book offers valuable insights, practical advice, and inspiration to those interested in exploring the world of publishing and embarking on their own entrepreneurial journey within it.

Market Research And Analysis

Market research and analysis are critical aspects of starting a publishing company. This process entails gathering and analyzing data on the publishing industry, target market, competitors, and customer preferences in order to make strategic decisions and improve the chances of success.

To begin, aspiring publishers should look into the current state of the publishing industry. This entails analyzing industry-wide trends, issues, and opportunities, such as the rise of digital publishing, shifting consumer preferences, and the development of distribution structures. By staying current on industry advancements, ambitious publishers can position themselves to capitalize on emerging trends and respond to changes in the publishing landscape.

Aspiring publishers should conduct target market research to better understand their audience's needs, preferences, and behavior. This includes identifying their target readership's demographics, psychographics, and purchasing patterns, as well as assessing their reading habits, preferences for specific genres or formats, and willingness to pay for material.

Prospective publishers who have a thorough understanding of their target market can efficiently adjust their publishing strategy to meet the needs and preferences of their audience. Prospective publishers should also conduct competition research to gain a better understanding of the competitive landscape and identify opportunities for differentiation.

This includes identifying current publishing companies that operate in the same category or genre, as well as evaluating their strengths, weaknesses, tactics, and market positioning. A competitive study enables aspiring publishers to identify market gaps, assess potential risks, and develop strategies for differentiating their publishing company and gaining a competitive advantage.

Aspiring publishers should conduct research on customer preferences and trends to inform their content acquisition and publication strategies. This includes analyzing data on popular genres, themes, and subjects, as well as identifying reader trends and preferences. Prospective publishers can make informed decisions about what types of material to buy, produce, and market to their target audience if they stay up-to-date on consumer preferences and trends.

Market research and analysis are critical steps in starting a publishing company. Prospective publishers can make informed decisions and create a strategic publishing strategy that maximizes their chances of success by gathering and analyzing data about the publishing industry, target market, competitors, and consumer preferences. By investing time and effort in market research and analysis, ambitious publishers can position themselves to thrive in today's competitive and dynamic publishing environment.

Developing a Business Strategy

Developing a business strategy is an important step in starting a publishing company. A well-crafted business plan serves as a road map for your company, outlining your goals, strategies, and financial projections.

This is a comprehensive guide to creating a business plan for your publishing company.

1. Executive Summary: Give a brief overview of your publishing company's goals, vision, and objectives.

Summarize key business plan components such as target market, competitor analysis, marketing strategy, and financial projections.

2. Firm Description: Provide specific information about your publishing company, such as its legal structure, location, and ownership. Describe the publishing niche or genres in which you wish to specialize, as well as any unique features or value propositions provided by your company.

3. Market Analysis: Conduct a thorough investigation into the publishing industry, identifying trends, obstacles, and potential opportunities. Identify and describe your target market's demographics, interests, and buying habits. Examine the competitive environment, including current publishing companies' strengths, weaknesses, and market positioning.

4. Outline your publishing company's organizational structure, including key personnel, roles, and responsibilities. Highlight your management team's qualifications and experience, as well as any advisers or consultants you intend to hire.

5. Product Line or Services: Describe your publishing company's offerings, such as genres, formats, and distribution channels. Provide information about your content acquisition strategy, including how you intend to find manuscripts or content authors.

6. Marketing and Sales Strategy: Develop a marketing strategy that includes tactics for promoting publications and growing your brand. Describe your sales strategy, including distribution channels, pricing strategies, and sales projections.

7. Financial Projections: Prepare detailed financial projections for your publishing company, including startup costs, revenue forecasts, and expense estimates. Include a break-even analysis and cash flow projections to demonstrate the financial viability of your business.

8. Determine your financial requirements and sources, such as personal savings, loans, and investors. Outline your financial strategy, including how you want to spend the money and when you plan to repay the loan.

9. Appendices: Include any additional information or proof that supports your company's plan, such as market research results, essential staff resumes, or legal documents.

10. Review and adjust your business strategy on a frequent basis to reflect your publishing company's expansion. Seek guidance from consultants, mentors, and industry professionals to ensure that your company's plan is comprehensive and viable. As your publishing company expands, review and revise the business plan, which is a live document.

Legal and financial considerations

When launching a publishing firm, it is necessary to consider both legal and financial problems. Navigating numerous legal requirements, preserving intellectual property, and adopting solid financial procedures are all important factors for the success and long-term survival of any publishing enterprise.

When beginning a publishing firm, there are various legal issues. First and foremost, you must decide on a legal form for your business, such as a sole proprietorship, partnership, corporation, or limited liability company (LLC). Each structure has distinct legal ramifications in terms of responsibility, taxation, and management flexibility, so choose the one that best suits your needs and objectives.

Once you've settled on a legal structure, you must register your publishing firm with the appropriate government agencies in your area. This might entail obtaining a business license, registering your firm name, and applying for any required permissions or certificates. Furthermore, you may need to comply with certain publishing industry rules and licensing requirements, such as getting an ISBN (International Standard Book Number) for your books. Intellectual property protection is a significant legal factor for publishing organizations.

This covers both copyright protection for your company's creative works and licensing arrangements for any third-party content you publish. You should also provide writers and content producers with explicit terms and conditions for copyright ownership, royalties, and rights management. Starting a publishing firm necessitates rigorous financial planning and management to ensure the long-term survival of your enterprise.

You will need to develop a comprehensive business plan that includes initial expenses, revenue predictions, and spending estimates. This can help you determine how much financing you'll need to start your publishing firm and how you'll distribute resources to meet operating expenditures like editorial, design, printing, marketing, and distribution. In addition to beginning expenditures, you'll need to budget for continuing expenses such as staff pay, rent, utilities, and other overhead costs connected with running a publishing business.

It is vital to develop a budget and financial predictions that represent these continuing costs while also taking into consideration prospective revenue and spending swings over time. In addition, you will need to establish financial systems and processes for tracking income and spending, managing cash flow, and ensuring tax compliance.

This might include installing accounting software, engaging an accountant or bookkeeper, and creating internal controls to secure financial assets and prevent fraud or misappropriation of cash. Finally, you should look at funding sources for your publishing firm. This might involve leveraging personal resources, acquiring loans or lines of credit from financial institutions, seeking investment from venture capitalists or angel investors, or raising funds through crowdsourcing platforms such as Kickstarter or Indiegogo.

Consider the advantages and disadvantages of each funding source before determining which one best meets your publishing company's financial needs and goals.

Skills And Competencies Needed For The Business

Preparing for entrepreneurship in publishing entails developing specific skills and competencies that are necessary for business success. These may include strong communication and negotiating skills for collaborating with writers and content creators, as well as editorial skills for reading and revising manuscripts to ensure quality and coherence.

Marketing and sales skills are required to promote publications and secure distribution channels, while project management skills are required to oversee the production process and meet deadlines.

Potential entrepreneurs must develop resilience, adaptability, and creativity in order to navigate the challenges and uncertainties of the publishing industry. Accepting failure as a learning opportunity, staying up-to-date on industry trends and advancements, and constantly seeking new ideas and techniques to stay competitive in the ever-changing publishing landscape are all part of this.

Entrepreneurs must establish a network of mentors, advisers, and industry experts who can offer advice, support, and valuable insights into the publishing industry. This network may include fellow entrepreneurs, industry groups, literary agents, and publishing specialists who can offer advice on everything from business development and content acquisition to marketing and distribution strategies. Finally, preparing for entrepreneurship in publishing requires a commitment to lifelong learning and professional development.

This includes staying current on industry trends, attending conferences and seminars, and seeking out opportunities for additional education and training in areas relevant to publishing entrepreneurship. Prospective entrepreneurs can position themselves for success by consistently investing in their talents, expertise, and networks and establishing a publishing firm that thrives in the competitive publishing sector

Let us go over the most important aspects of publishing entrepreneurship preparation.

1. **Self-assessment:** Think about your strengths, weaknesses, and goals to determine whether you're ready for entrepreneurship.

2. **Market research** involves analyzing industry trends, customer preferences, and competition to identify niche opportunities.

3. Determine the company's vision, goals, and strategies for acquiring, producing, distributing, marketing, and selling content.

4. **Legal and financial considerations:** select an appropriate legal structure, obtain any necessary licenses, follow copyright regulations, and develop a financial strategy.

5. **Ability development:** Improve communication, negotiation, editorial, marketing, sales, and project management skills, all of which are essential for publishing success.

6. Mindset development: value resilience, adaptability, and creativity in order to overcome obstacles and uncertainties in entrepreneurship.

7. Establish a network of mentors, advisers, and industry professionals who can offer advice, support, and insights. 8. Lifelong learning: Stay current on industry advances, attend conferences and workshops, and seek additional education and training to remain competitive.

Things To Consider Before Starting a Publishing Company

Before embarking on the journey of starting a publishing company, you must first assess your skills and interests to ensure that they are compatible with the demands of publishing entrepreneurship.

This test includes a thorough evaluation of your personal characteristics and professional abilities, as well as an examination of your enthusiasm and commitment to the publishing industry.

Begin by thinking about your own characteristics and traits that are relevant to publishing entrepreneurship. Consider your level of inventiveness, attention to detail, and communication abilities.

Assess your organizational skills, time management abilities, and willingness to take the initiative and lead initiatives. Evaluate your resilience, adaptability, and willingness to face the uncertainties and challenges that come with entrepreneurship.

Next, assess your professional abilities and publishing-related knowledge. Evaluate your understanding of the publishing industry's trends, challenges, and opportunities. Consider your experience with different publication formats, distribution networks, and marketing strategies.

Evaluate your editing skills, including your ability to examine and criticize manuscripts, provide constructive feedback to writers, and ensure the quality and coherence of published works.

Also, evaluate your marketing and sales abilities, including your ability to promote publications, secure distribution channels, and generate revenue. Think about your passion for and interest in publishing.

Consider your interest in reading, writing, and the creative arts, and assess your willingness to contribute to the cultural and intellectual environment through publication.

Consider your commitment to promoting diversity and inclusion in publishing, as well as your encouragement of new authors and underrepresented perspectives.

Consider your long-term publishing sector goals and aspirations, as well as your desire to invest time, effort, and resources in the growth of a successful publishing company.

When evaluating your skills and interests in relation to starting a publishing company, it is critical to be honest and realistic about your strengths and areas for growth.

Consider seeking feedback from mentors, advisers, and industry experts to gain new ideas and perspectives. By thoroughly examining your skills and interests, you can gain clarity and confidence in your decision to pursue publishing entrepreneurship, laying the groundwork for success in the dynamic and lucrative world of publishing.

Establishing your publishing company is a huge undertaking that necessitates several crucial steps and considerations. Here is a detailed guide to help you navigate the process:

1. Define Your Vision: Begin by describing your vision for the publishing company. What type of content do you wish to publish? What are the company's goals and objectives? Clarifying your vision will help guide your decisions and activities as you establish and grow your publishing company.

2. Choose a business structure: Decide whether your publishing company will be a sole proprietorship, partnership, corporation, or limited liability company (LLC). Each structure has benefits and disadvantages in terms of responsibility, taxes, and management flexibility; therefore, choose the one that best suits your needs and goals.

3. Register Your Business: Make sure you register your publishing company with the appropriate government officials in your area. This may entail obtaining a business license, registering your company's name, and applying for any necessary approvals or certifications.

4. Set up Your Office: Create a physical or virtual office space for your publishing enterprise. This might include setting up a home office, renting commercial office space, or utilizing co-working spaces. Make certain that your office space has all of the equipment and tools you'll require to run your publishing firm, such as computers, printers, and internet access.

5. Build Your Brand: Create a strong and distinct brand identity for your publishing company. This includes choosing a name, designing a logo, and developing branding

materials such as business cards, letterheads, and websites. Your brand identity should reflect your publishing company's beliefs, aims, and vision while also appealing to your target audience.

6. Begin accumulating material for your publishing company. This might involve seeking manuscripts from authors, acquiring rights to previously published works, or commissioning content from freelance writers. Create a clear content acquisition strategy that aligns with your publication's aims and target audience.

7. Build Your Team: As your publishing company grows, you may need to put together a team of pros to help with operations. This might include editors, designers, marketers, salesmen, and administrative professionals. Hire people who share your passion for publishing and have the skills and experience needed to help your firm succeed.

8. Create publishing processes: Set up publishing processes and workflows to streamline your operations. This might comprise editorial procedures for manuscript review and editing, production processes for formatting and layout, and printing and distribution processes. Establish clear

guidelines and standards to ensure consistency and quality in your published outputs.

9. Create a Marketing Plan: Develop a comprehensive marketing strategy to promote your publications and create your brand. This might include strategies for online and offline marketing, social media marketing, email marketing, content marketing, and public relations. Identify your target audience, craft an engaging message, and choose the most effective marketing platforms to reach them.

10. Determine Distribution Channels: Consider how you will distribute your material to viewers. This might include collaborating with bookstores, libraries, online merchants, and distributors, as well as selling directly to customers through your own website and other online platforms. Create distribution agreements and collaborations to increase the reach and accessibility of your articles.

11. Establish Your Publishing Business: After you've completed all of the essential procedures, you may formally establish your publishing business. This might involve hosting a launch event, publicizing your company's debut through press releases and social media, and advertising

your first pieces to generate excitement and interest among readers.

12. Monitor and Adapt: Keep track of your publishing company's progress and be prepared to change your strategy and operations as necessary. Stay current on industry trends, consumer tastes, and emerging technologies to keep your publishing company competitive and relevant in an ever-changing publishing landscape. Following these processes and considerations will assist you in establishing a solid foundation for your publishing company and positioning yourself for success in the competitive and dynamic publishing business.

Business Model Approach in Publishing

When starting a publishing company, selecting the right expertise and developing a sustainable business model are crucial for defining your company's focus and guaranteeing its long-term success.

First thing to consider are:

Niche Selection: Selecting the right niche is crucial for a publishing company since it defines your target audience, differentiates your offerings, and builds your brand identity. When settling on a niche, consider your own interests, expertise, and excitement.

Are you drawn to fiction or nonfiction? Is there a genre or subject about which you are particularly passionate? Identifying a specialty that is relevant to your hobbies and experience may make the publishing process more enjoyable while also increasing your chances of success.

Consider market demand and trends while choosing a specialty.

Discover popular genres, new trends, and underrepresented communities in the publishing industry. Look for market gaps where your publishing business may provide unique and relevant content.

By selecting a high-demand sector with limited competition, you may position your publishing company for success and establish a loyal fan base. Think about the size and growth possibilities of your chosen specialization.

Is it a large and growing niche, or a smaller, more specialized market? While larger niches may provide better earning possibilities, smaller niches sometimes have fewer rivals and are easier to establish a presence in.

When determining the size and development potential of your chosen niche, take into account your resources, capabilities, and long-term objectives.

Business Model: Once you've identified a niche, you'll need to develop a business plan that aligns with your publishing goals and objectives.

When starting a publishing company, there are several business models to choose from, each with its own set of rewards and obstacles.

In a traditional publishing model, the publishing company buys manuscripts from writers, edits and designs them, prints physical copies of the book, and distributes them to bookstores, libraries, and other retail locations. The publisher compensates the author through royalties, depending on book sales. This technique requires a significant upfront investment in editing, design, printing, and distribution, but it has the potential to enhance book sales revenue.

Self-Publishing: The self-publishing approach gives writers entire control over the publishing process, including editing, design, printing, and distribution of their works. Authors can self-publish their works using platforms like Amazon Kindle Direct Publishing (KDP) and Ingram Spark.

This technique allows writers greater creative freedom and flexibility, but it also requires them to invest time and resources in marketing and promotion in order to reach their target audience.

Hybrid publication: This publication approach combines elements of traditional publishing with self-publishing. Hybrid publisher work with writers to develop and distribute books, but authors may be required to pay for editing, design, and distribution. Depending on the author's requirements and preferences, hybrid publishers may offer a wide range of services, such as editing, design, marketing, and distribution.

This method gives authors more assistance and resources than self-publishing, although it may necessitate an upfront financial investment. Determine the ideal business model for your publishing firm by taking into account your specialty, goals, available resources, and target audience.

Consider the pros and cons of each model before deciding which one best matches your publishing strategy and goals. By selecting the right niche and developing an effective business plan, you can provide a solid foundation for your publishing company and position yourself for success in the competitive and dynamic publishing industry.

Setting up of office space

Setting up an office is an important stage in launching a publishing firm. Your office is the hub for daily operations, team communication, and company activity.

Here's a detailed guide to organizing your office space:

Location: Select an office location that suits your demands and fits your budget. Consider the location's accessibility, amenities, and possible clients or collaborators. You may save money by working from home, renting a commercial office space for a professional atmosphere, or using co-working spaces for flexibility and networking. Design an office arrangement that maximizes productivity and efficiency.

Arrange furniture and equipment to create suitable workstations for a variety of activities, such as writing, editing, design, and administration. Consider ergonomic concepts to safeguard your own and your team's comfort and well-being. Purchase the essential equipment and furniture for your publishing activities.

This might include computers, printers, scanners, ergonomic seats, desks, filing cabinets, and storage solutions. Choose high-quality, long-lasting equipment that meets your requirements and budget.

Technology: Create the required technology infrastructure to support your publishing efforts. Ensure that you have stable internet access, enough bandwidth, and cybersecurity procedures in place to secure important data. Consider investing in publishing software, project management tools, and communication platforms to improve productivity and cooperation.

Create a collection of reference materials, industry publications, and resources to supplement your publishing efforts. Stock up on books, journals, style guides, and reference materials related to your expertise and publication objectives. Consider subscribing to internet databases and research tools to have access to a diverse set of resources. Meeting Spaces: Set aside meeting spaces in your workplace for team meetings, client meetings, and collaborative sessions. To support talks and brainstorming sessions, equip meeting rooms with presentation technology like projectors and whiteboards. Consider creating a pleasant and attractive workplace to encourage creativity and cooperation. Implement smart storage and organization solutions to keep your workplace space clean and efficient.

To keep books, manuscripts, papers, and office supplies organized, use shelving systems, file cabinets, and storage containers. Label objects and create file systems so that materials can be quickly located and accessed when needed. Decor and atmosphere: Make your working environment seem friendly and exciting.

Decorate with artwork, plants, and other things that reflect your publishing company's identity and beliefs. Consider using natural light, pleasant seating places, and break rooms to improve employee well-being and creativity.

Accessibility: Make your workplace area accessible to everyone, including those with impairments. Install ramps, elevators, and accessible restrooms to assist those with mobility issues. Consider ergonomic design ideas to make your office more pleasant and inclusive for all team members.

Prioritize safety and security in your business environment. Implement fire extinguishers, smoke detectors, first aid kits, and emergency evacuation procedures to ensure occupant safety. Install security equipment, such as alarms and video cameras, to keep your workplace and valuables safe from theft or damage.

Finally, setting up your office space is a critical component of launching a publishing firm. By carefully planning and designing your office layout, investing in appropriate equipment and technology, establishing a welcoming environment, and prioritizing safety and security, you can create a productive and exciting workspace that will help your publishing endeavor succeed.

Understanding the State of the Publishing Industry

Understanding the current state of the publishing industry is crucial for anybody thinking about starting a publishing firm. In recent years, the industry has experienced significant upheaval as a result of technological advancements, changes in customer behavior, and distribution pattern changes

Digital publishing has emerged as one of the most significant advances in the publishing industry. E-books and audiobooks are gaining popularity among readers, forcing a shift away from traditional print publications. The increasing usage of e-readers, tablets, and smartphones has accelerated this trend, making digital reading more accessible and convenient. Another noteworthy development is the growing popularity of self-publishing.

Technological improvements have democratized the publishing process, allowing authors to bypass traditional publishers and self-publish their work. Self-publishing platforms such as Amazon Kindle Direct Publishing (KDP) and Smash-words have allowed authors to connect directly with readers, resulting in a surge in self-published works across a wide range of genres.

The publishing industry has seen a surge in niche and independent publishing businesses that cater to certain genres, interests, and underrepresented groups. These niche publishers focus on certain markets, such as genre fiction, academic publishing, or regional interests, and may employ a more specialized and targeted approach to content acquisition, production, and marketing. In addition to digital and self-publishing, the publishing industry has experienced changes in distribution systems.

Brick-and-mortar bookstores have faltered due to competition from online retailers such as Amazon and the growing popularity of e-books. Independent bookstores, on the other hand, have had a revival in recent years, owing to community support and an emphasis on carefully curated selections and author events.

Audiobooks have emerged as a key development segment for the publishing company. Consumers now have more access to and convenience with audiobooks because of developments in audio technology and the proliferation of smartphones. The audiobook market has risen substantially in recent years as publishers and writers have increased their investment in audio production and distribution. Despite these advancements, conventional publishing organizations continue to play an essential role in the publishing sector.

Enormous publishing businesses dominate the sector due to their enormous distribution networks, marketing resources, and existing author ties. However, independent publishers and self-publishing writers have carved out a niche for themselves by offering customers a broad range of material while also driving industry innovation.

To recap, the publishing business is facing considerable upheaval as a result of technological discoveries, modifications in consumer behavior, and new distribution systems. Understanding the present condition of the publishing business is crucial for anybody contemplating launching a publishing firm, as it informs strategic decision-making and identifies chances for innovation and progress in this dynamic and competitive sector.

Anyone looking to start a publishing company must first understand the industry's trends and challenges. These trends and challenges shape the competitive landscape and influence ambitious publishers' strategic decisions. Digital publishing has emerged as one of the most significant changes in the publishing industry.

Readers are increasingly turning away from traditional printed publications in favor of e-books, audiobooks, and digital platforms. Technological advancements, changes in consumer behavior, and the increased availability of digital reading devices have all contributed to this trend. Self-publishing is also becoming increasingly popular.

Technological advancements have democratized the publishing process, allowing authors to self-publish their works through platforms like Amazon Kindle Direct Publishing (KDP) and Smash-words. Self-publishing has allowed authors to bypass traditional publishing houses and contact readers directly, resulting in a surge of self-published novels across a variety of genres. Furthermore, niche publishing has become a significant market trend.

Niche publishers focus on niche genres, hobbies, or underrepresented populations, catering to markets such as genre fiction, academic publishing, and regional interests. These niche publishers frequently adopt a more focused and targeted approach to content acquisition, production, and marketing, allowing them to stand out in a crowded market.

Despite these changes, potential publishers face a number of challenges. One of the most significant issues is competition from digital platforms and online businesses. Brick-and-mortar bookstores have struggled due to competition from online retailers such as Amazon, which has disrupted traditional distribution patterns and altered customer purchasing habits. Another challenge is the ever-changing landscape of copyright and intellectual property rights.

As publishing becomes more digitally focused, concerns about copyright infringement, piracy, and digital rights management have grown. Aspiring publishers must address these legal and ethical concerns in order to protect their intellectual property and ensure fair compensation for authors and content creators.

Challenges in the Publishing Industry

The publishing industry faces challenges with diversity and inclusion.

There is a growing demand for diverse perspectives and representation in literature, and publishers are under pressure to diversify their catalogs and editorial staff.

To remain relevant and inclusive in a rapidly changing world, aspiring publishers must embrace diversity and inclusion initiatives.

Furthermore, the publishing industry is vulnerable to economic pressures and market fluctuations. Publishers face challenges such as fluctuating book sales, rising manufacturing costs, and changing customer preferences. To ensure that their publishing operations are financially sustainable, aspiring publishers must develop adaptable business models that can respond to changing market conditions.

Finally, anyone interested in starting a publishing company should understand the industry's trends and problems. Aspiring publishers should position themselves for success in today's dynamic and competitive world by staying current on industry developments, capitalizing on digital publishing opportunities, resolving legal and ethical issues, and negotiating financial constraints.

The Potential of the Publishing Industry

Understanding the potential of the publishing industry is critical for anyone thinking about starting a publishing company. These prospects can help prospective publishers identify opportunities for business growth, innovation, and differentiation. The expansion of digital publishing presents a significant opportunity for the publishing industry.

E-books, audiobooks, and digital platforms have opened up new possibilities for content distribution and consumption. Aspiring publishers should seize this opportunity by embracing digital publishing formats and platforms, broadening their reach, and adapting to changing consumer preferences for digital reading experiences.

Self-publishing's popularity enables prospective publishers to collaborate with independent writers and content providers. Publishers can help self-published authors reach a larger audience by providing publishing services such as editing, design, and distribution. This collaboration can lead to mutually beneficial partnerships and revenue-sharing opportunities.

Niche publishing allows potential publishers to target specific genres, interests, or underrepresented groups. Publishers can differentiate themselves from larger competitors and build a loyal following by focusing on niche markets such as genre literature, academic publishing, or regional interests. Particular publishing allows publishers to target specific interests and create unique content that resonates with specific audiences.

Furthermore, audiobooks are a growing segment of the publishing industry, giving publishers the opportunity to diversify their content offerings. Consumers now have more access to and convenience with audiobooks because of developments in audio technology and the proliferation of smartphones. Aspiring publishers can capitalize on this trend by producing and distributing audiobooks alongside traditional print and e-book formats, thereby reaching audiobook listeners and expanding their audience base.

Foreign growth enables publishers to reach global audiences and increase their market share. Publishers can now disseminate their publications internationally and reach readers in a variety of countries and areas, thanks to the proliferation of digital distribution channels and online stores. Translating and customizing material for international markets allows publishers to broaden their global reach and increase their revenue.

The growing desire for diverse perspectives and representation in literature presents an opportunity for publishers to support diversity and inclusion initiatives. Publishers can reach a large audience by publishing diverse writers and content that reflects a wide range of experiences and opinions. Embracing diversity and inclusion may create new opportunities for collaboration and audience participation.

Content acquisition and management

Content acquisition and management are critical aspects of starting a publishing company. To build a diverse and appealing publication library, aspiring publishers must establish effective content acquisition, evaluation, and management procedures. Content acquisition entails collecting manuscripts, books, and other intellectual property for publication. This procedure may include soliciting submissions from writers, agencies, and content providers, as well as acquiring rights to previously published works.

Aspiring publishers must have a clear content acquisition strategy that aligns with their publishing goals, target audience, and specialized market. When acquiring material, publishers must consider factors such as quality, marketability, and consistency with their publication strategy. Publishers should evaluate manuscripts and proposals on the basis of originality, writing quality, relevance to the intended audience, and financial viability.

Maintaining a balance between acquiring well-known writers and discovering new talent is critical for keeping the publishing catalog fresh and diverse. Publishers must efficiently manage the editorial and production processes in order to ensure high-quality publications after purchasing materials. This includes assigning editors, proofreaders, and designers to work on manuscripts, managing production schedules, and overseeing the entire production process, from manuscript to finished product.

Publishers must maintain open lines of communication with writers and content producers throughout the editorial and production process in order to resolve any issues and ensure the realization of their magazine's vision. In addition to acquiring and managing content for publication, publishers must deal with rights management and licensing issues.

This includes negotiating contracts with writers, agencies, and content creators, obtaining copyright authorization, and overseeing rights for digital distribution, translation, and adaptation.

Publishers must ensure that they possess the necessary rights and permits to publish and distribute material in a variety of formats and countries. Furthermore, content management entails keeping track of publications as well as managing rights and revenues from published works. Publishers must establish systems and processes for cataloging and categorizing publications, tracking sales and royalties, and managing author contracts and payments.

Consider implementing digital asset management systems, royalty tracking tools, and rights management databases to improve content management efficiency. Overall, effective content acquisition and management are essential to the success of any publishing company.

Developing a clear content acquisition strategy, acquiring high-quality content, effectively managing the editorial and production processes, and implementing rights management and royalties systems allow aspiring publishers to create a diverse and compelling catalog of publications that resonate with their target audience and contribute to the success and growth of their publishing venture.

Publishers must prioritize not only content acquisition and maintenance but also content curation and positioning. This entails creating a distinct brand identity and an editorial voice that resonates with the target audience. Publishers should choose a catalog that maintains a consistent brand message and allows customers to identify with the publishing company's beliefs and themes.

Content curation also entails making strategic decisions about article sequence and scheduling. Publishers must consider market trends, seasonal demand, and potential synergies between products in their portfolio. Publishers can maximize their impact, gain a larger readership, and capitalize on market opportunities by properly organizing their publishing releases.

Content management necessitates effective marketing and promotion. Publishers should develop effective marketing strategies to increase the visibility, interest, and sales of their publications. This could entail using a variety of channels, including social media, email marketing, book reviews, author interviews, and participation in literary events. Establishing strong partnerships with bookstores, libraries, and online merchants is essential for effective distribution and market presence.

In the era of digital publishing, publishers should consider new formats and platforms. This could entail using e-books, audiobooks, and interactive digital content to cater to a wide range of reader preferences. Experimenting with different formats can help the publisher expand its reach and generate new revenue.

Author connections are critical for effective content management. Publishers should maintain open lines of communication with writers and incorporate them into the editorial and promotional processes. Building strong relationships with writers enhances the publishing experience, inspires loyalty, and can lead to long-term collaborations.

Finally, content acquisition and management are critical components of any successful publishing business. Publishers can create a diverse and appealing catalog by implementing effective content acquisition, evaluation, and management procedures.

Comprehensive content management entails content curation, strategic positioning, marketing activities, the exploration of innovative formats, and the formation of strong author relationships, all of which contribute to a publishing venture's overall success and longevity.

Acquiring rights and permissions

Acquiring rights and permissions is an important step in starting a publishing company because it requires a legal license to publish and distribute information. This procedure applies to a broad range of rights, including copyright licenses, translation rights, adaptation rights, and digital rights, among others.

When acquiring rights, publishers must first locate the rights holders and negotiate license agreements outlining the terms and limitations on usage. This typically entails negotiating with writers, agents, literary estates, and other rights holders to obtain the necessary permissions.

Negotiations may include a variety of topics, including royalty rates, regional rights, format rights, and the term of rights. Copyright permits are one of the most common rights that publishers must obtain. Copyright grants the author of an original work exclusive rights to its use and distribution. Before duplicating, distributing, or exhibiting a work in print, digital, or other media, publishers must obtain permission from the copyright holder, who is usually the author or their representative.

In addition to copyright licenses, publishers may need to get translation rights in order to publish works in many languages. Translation rights allow publishers to translate and publish works in languages other than the original language of publication. Obtaining translation rights sometimes requires reaching agreements with writers or their agents to secure the right to translate and publish the work in certain languages and areas. Adaptation rights allow you to adapt a work into several media or forms, such as film, television, theater, or graphic novels.

Publishers that want to adapt works must secure adaptation rights from the rights holders and sign agreements specifying the criteria of adaptation, such as payment, creative control, and distribution rights. Digital rights encompass the capacity to create and distribute works in digital media, such as e-books, audiobooks, and digital platforms.

With the rise of digital publishing, publishers must increasingly prioritize protecting digital rights. This might include making agreements with writers, agencies, and other rights holders to obtain permission to publish and distribute works in digital formats through online stores, e-book platforms, and audiobook platforms. In addition to gaining rights for individual works, publishers must handle collective rights for anthologies, compilations, and other group works.

This entails obtaining permission from various copyright holders for works included in a collection, as well as establishing agreements that outline the collective work's terms of use and distribution. When requesting permissions and approvals, publishers must follow copyright laws and intellectual property rights constraints.

This includes conducting due diligence to determine the rights status of works, documenting licenses and agreements in writing, and getting legal help as needed to deal with complicated legal issues. Overall, obtaining rights and permissions is a vital step in starting a publishing company since it requires legal authorization to print and distribute material. Publishers may obtain the licenses they require to develop a diverse and compelling library of publications by understanding the many types of rights, reaching agreements with rights holders, and ensuring compliance with copyright laws and regulations.

Managing authors and content producers

Managing authors and content producers is a crucial aspect of starting a publishing company since it necessitates building solid relationships, encouraging collaboration, and ensuring the success of published works. Effective management of authors and content creators increases overall publication quality, enhances the publishing company's reputation, and fosters a positive and productive work environment.

One of the most crucial components of managing authors and content creators is to establish clear communication channels and maintain regular contact throughout the publication process. Publishers should have open lines of contact with authors and content suppliers, providing frequent updates on editorial input, production timelines, marketing plans, and other relevant information.

Clear and honest communication builds trust and collaboration between publishers and writers, ensuring that everyone is on the same page and working towards common goals. Furthermore, publishers must aid and guide authors and content creators throughout the publishing process. This may involve offering editorial feedback, manuscript development help, and publishing aid.

Publishers should act as mentors and advocates for their writers, providing resources, support, and constructive criticism to help authors realize their creative visions and achieve their publishing goals. In addition to offering help, publishers are responsible for managing contractual agreements with writers and content suppliers.

This includes creating contract terms, identifying rights and permissions, and ensuring legal and contractual compliance. Publishers should develop fair and transparent contracts that outline both parties' rights, obligations, and pay arrangements, creating a mutually beneficial collaboration based on trust and respect. Publishers also play a significant role in promoting the work of authors and content providers to increase visibility and reach.

This includes developing comprehensive marketing and promotional strategies to showcase published works, increase exposure, and attract readers. Publishers should utilize a number of channels, including social media, book launches, author events, and media outreach, to generate buzz and interest in their writers' and content providers' works.

Managing authors and content producers means giving continuing assistance and advice beyond the publication of a single piece. Publishers should work closely with writers to enhance their careers by offering opportunities for more publications, collaborations, and professional development. By building long-term relationships with authors and content producers, publishers may build a loyal and talented pool of creators who contribute to the company's success and growth.

Overall, managing authors and content providers is a difficult process requiring effective communication, help, contractual administration, and promotional efforts. Publishers may foster creativity, innovation, and success by building strong relationships, providing guidance and support, managing contractual commitments, and promoting the work of authors and content suppliers.

Importance of Editing and quality control in Publishing

Editing and quality control are key components of starting a publishing company, as they ensure that published works meet the highest standards of excellence and professionalism. Effective editing and quality control methods increase a publishing company's overall quality, credibility, and reputation, as well as the reading experience for its customers.

Editing is the process of assessing and improving manuscript clarity, coherence, accuracy, and overall literary quality. This technique consists of multiple stages, each of which focuses on a different aspect of the work: developmental editing, substantive editing, copyediting, and proofreading.

Developmental editing assesses the manuscript's structure, substance, and organization and provides feedback on plot development, character development, pace, and overall narrative flow.

Developmental editors work directly with authors to enhance plots, character arcs, and structural issues, resulting in a compelling and engaging reading experience.

Substantive editing focuses on improving the manuscript's substance and style, including language use, tone, voice, and consistency. Substantive editors try to clarify complex concepts, improve readability, and ensure content coherence and consistency. They may also suggest changes to improve clarity, decrease redundancy, and boost overall coherence. Copyediting is the act of fine-tuning a manuscript's language and style, with a focus on grammar, punctuation, spelling, syntax, and other technical aspects of writing.

Copyeditors meticulously review manuscripts to eradicate errors, improve readability, and ensure adherence to style guidelines and editorial standards. They also check for consistency in formatting, citations, and references to provide a professional and polished appearance.

Proofreading, the final phase in the editing process, involves identifying and correcting errors in spelling, punctuation, grammar, and formatting. Proofreaders extensively examine the manuscript before publication to identify any remaining defects or inconsistencies, ensuring that the final product is error-free and ready for print or digital distribution. In addition to editing, quality control activities involve rigorous inspections to ensure that published works meet the highest quality and professionalism standards.

Peer review, fact-checking, accuracy verification, and adhering to ethical and legal standards are all possible quality control methods. Peer review is the practice of soliciting feedback from other subject-matter experts or professionals in order to evaluate the quality, correctness, and usefulness of the information.

Peer reviewers provide valuable insights and recommendations for improvement, ensuring that published works meet professional standards and contribute to the advancement of knowledge in their respective fields. Fact-checkers thoroughly review the content to ensure that all statements, statistics, and references are accurate and supported by credible sources.

Quality control procedures include respect for ethical and legal norms, such as copyright compliance, plagiarism detection, and adherence to editorial rules and industry best practices. Fact-checkers rigorously evaluate the material to ensure its accuracy and identify any flaws or discrepancies that require correction. Publishers must ensure that published works respect the intellectual property rights of writers and content creators, follow copyright laws, and uphold high ethical and professional standards.

Publishing methods and distribution

Publishing methods and distribution are critical components of starting a publishing company, since they encompass the multiple stages required to bring a book from draft to market and make it available to consumers. The publishing process starts with the purchase of manuscripts or material, then proceeds on to editing, design, production, and marketing, before eventually distributing to merchants and customers.

To guarantee timely and effective publication, each stage of the publishing process involves careful planning, organization, and execution. Editing is the act of analyzing and polishing manuscripts to improve their clarity, coherence, accuracy, and overall literary quality. This includes developmental editing, substantive editing, copyediting, and proofreading, with each focusing on a different aspect of the text to assure its readiness for publishing.

Design is essential for producing visually appealing and financially viable publications. This involves designing book covers, layouts, typefaces, and other visual elements to enhance the book's appearance and readability. Designers collaborate with writers and editors to create covers and layouts that reflect the tone, genre, and content of the book while also appealing to the target audience.

Production includes printing, formatting, and binding publications for physical distribution. Publishers work with printing companies to provide high-quality printed editions of their publications that meet industry standards for printing, paper, and binding. In addition to physical production, publishers create e-books and audiobooks for digital distribution. This includes translating manuscripts to digital formats, optimizing them for e-book readers and audiobook platforms, and making sure they work with a variety of devices and software.

Marketing is crucial for boosting notoriety, attention, and money for publications. Publishers develop comprehensive marketing strategies that may include both online and offline marketing tactics, such as social media marketing, email marketing, book reviews, author interviews, book signings, and attendance at literary events. Marketing strategies aim to attract the target audience and raise awareness of publications, resulting in increased sales and profits. Distribution comprises making publications available to merchants, wholesalers, libraries, and readers through various distribution channels.

Publishers work with distributors, wholesalers, and retailers to ensure that their publications are accessible for purchase in physical and online bookstores, libraries, and other retail venues. Distribution efforts aim to broaden the reach and accessibility of publications, making them available to readers wherever they purchase books.

Publishing methods and distribution are critical components of establishing a publishing company, covering the multiple stages required in bringing a book from draft to market and making it available to readers. Publishers may successfully launch and promote their publications by effectively managing the editing, design, production, marketing, and distribution processes, allowing them to reach their target audience and achieve their publishing goals.

Differences between Print media and Digital Way of Publishing

When starting a publishing firm, it's important to understand the many types of publishing accessible, such as print and digital. Each has its own set of advantages and disadvantages that potential publishers should evaluate.

Print publishing involves making physical copies of books, magazines, and other printed materials. This traditional method of publication has been around for centuries and remains popular today, despite the rise of digital publishing.

Print books provide several practical advantages, including the tactile experience of holding a tangible book, the ability to annotate and bookmark pages, and the visual appeal of printed covers and designs.

Print publishing also enables its distribution in physical bookstores, libraries, and other retail establishments.

However, print publication requires upfront costs for printing, distribution, and inventory management, as well as environmental considerations concerning paper use and waste.

Digital publishing, on the other hand, is the process of developing electronic copies of books, periodicals, or other materials for use on digital devices such as e-readers, tablets, and smartphones.

Digital publishing offers several benefits over print publishing, including lower production costs, faster distribution via online platforms, and the ability to reach a global audience quickly. E-books and digital magazines are often less expensive to make and distribute than print publications, making them a popular choice among self-publishers and independent authors.

Furthermore, digital publication allows for innovative features like hyperlinks, multimedia content, and interactive elements to enhance the reading experience.

However, digital publication brings a number of challenges, including formatting difficulties across several devices and platforms, worries about digital rights management and piracy, and the need for continuous digital file updates and maintenance. In recent years, hybrid publishing approaches have emerged, combining elements of print and digital publication.

These techniques allow you to publish content in a number of formats to satisfy the demands of different readers and markets. For example, some publishers provide "print-on-demand" services, in which physical copies of books are produced only when orders are received, reducing upfront costs and inventory management.

Other publishers use "e-book first" strategies, which entail publishing digital copies of books before or alongside print editions in order to attract digitally savvy consumers and capitalize on online distribution channels. Hybrid publishing strategies allow publishers to adapt to changing market trends and client preferences while expanding the reach and accessibility of their products.

Overall, aspiring publishers must understand the many types of publishing, including print and digital, before establishing a publishing company. By considering the advantages and disadvantages of each, publishers may make better-informed decisions about their publishing strategies and tailor their offerings to the needs and preferences of their target audience.

Whether employing print, digital, or hybrid publishing approaches, the goal is the same: to generate high-quality goods that captivate readers while also contributing to the publishing company's success and growth.

In addition, ambitious publishers must comprehend the ever-changing landscape of digital publishing formats and platforms. In addition to e-books, digital publishing includes audiobooks, online magazines, digital comics, and interactive storytelling experiences.

Each of these approaches offers a distinct opportunity for storytelling, creativity, and audience participation. Audiobooks, for example, have grown significantly in recent years, mainly due to advances in audio technology and the increased usage of smartphones and smart speakers.

Audiobooks enable users to consume books in an aural format, making them more accessible to busy people who prefer to listen while commuting, exercising, or multitasking.

Aspiring publishers can capitalize on the audiobook boom by producing high-quality audio recordings of their books and distributing them through audiobook services like Audible, iTunes, and Google Play. Other types of digital publications include online magazines and digital comics, which cater to specific reader demographics and interests.

Online magazines offer a platform for publishing articles, essays, and multimedia content on a wide range of topics, including lifestyle, fashion, technology, and culture. Publishers can use digital comics to distribute graphic novels, comic books, and web-comics in digital formats that are compatible with computers, tablets, and smartphones.

Aspiring publishers can experiment with different digital formats to broaden their publishing offerings and reach new audiences interested in visual storytelling and digital content consumption.

Furthermore, interactive storytelling experiences are a cutting-edge form of digital publishing that employs technology to engage readers in immersive and interactive narratives. Interactive storytelling platforms allow readers to participate in the story by making choices that influence the plot and ending. This revolutionary narrative style blurs the line between traditional literature and interactive media, offering readers a dynamic and personalized reading experience.

Aspiring publishers can experiment with interactive storytelling platforms to create unique and compelling storylines that capture readers' attention and distinguish their publishing company in the digital market. Finally, before starting a publishing company, aspiring publishers should understand the vast ecosystem of digital publishing formats and platforms. By researching the opportunities provided by digital publishing, publishers can broaden their publishing offerings, engage new audiences, and capitalize on growing trends in digital content consumption.

Whether using traditional print publishing, digital publishing, or hybrid publishing formats, the goal is to adapt to readers' changing wants and preferences while maintaining narrative quality and creativity.

Factors to be considered in each Printing Processes

Starting a publishing company, production and printing factors are important because they influence the quality, cost, and efficiency of producing physical copies of publications.

First and foremost, selecting the correct printing process is critical. The publishing industry uses two main processes: offset printing and digital printing. Offset printing is ideal for large print runs because it produces high-quality, cost-effective results in large quantities.

Digital printing, on the other hand, is ideal for shorter print runs because it offers greater flexibility, faster turnaround times, and cost-effectiveness for smaller quantities.

Understanding the advantages and disadvantages of each method is essential for making informed decisions about print volume, budget, and production timeline. Second, choosing the right paper stock is critical for achieving the desired look and feel of the finished product.

Consider the paper's weight, quality, color, and texture. For example, coated paper with a glossy finish may be preferred for bright colors and sharp images, whereas uncoated paper with a matte finish may be preferred for a more subdued and tactile aesthetic. Publishers should carefully select paper materials that are appropriate for the publication's content and target readership while also considering practical factors such as durability and cost.

Third, effective prepress process management is critical for producing accurate and high-quality printing results. Typesetting, layout design, color management, picture resolution, and file preparation are all part of the prepress process. Publishers should work closely with designers and prepress professionals to optimize files for printing, resolve any font or graphic issues, and ensure printer compatibility and specifications.

Attention to detail during the prepress process is essential for reducing errors and ensuring consistent print quality across multiple runs. Fourth, quality control during the printing process is essential for detecting and resolving any issues that may arise during production.

This includes performing press checks to ensure color accuracy, registration, and overall print quality before moving on to full production. It is critical to train press operators on how to identify and resolve common printing issues such as ink smudging, misalignment, and paper jams.

Furthermore, publishers may employ quality control measures such as color proofs, print samples, and random inspections to monitor print quality throughout the manufacturing process and ensure consistency and accuracy in the finished product.

Finally, managing post-production tasks such as binding, finishing, and packaging is critical to delivering a professional and marketable product. Publishers can choose binding methods such as perfect binding, saddle stitching, or case binding based on the publication format and design specifications.

Finishing options include lamination, embossing, foil stamping, and spot UV coating, which can improve the final product's visual appeal and durability. Publishers should also think about packaging and shipping logistics to ensure that printed copies arrive safely and securely at distribution points and customers.

Finally, when starting a publishing company, you must consider production and printing. Publishers can produce high-quality publications that meet readers' expectations while also contributing to their company's success and reputation by carefully selecting printing methods and paper stock, managing the prepress process, implementing quality control measures, and effectively managing post-production tasks.

Distribution channels and strategy

Distribution channels and strategy are important aspects of starting a publishing company because they affect how publications reach readers and consumers.

A successful distribution plan includes determining the best routes to reach the target audience, streamlining logistics and operations, and increasing publication exposure and accessibility. Traditional brick-and-mortar bookstores, which include independent bookstores, chain retailers, and specialty stores, are one of publishers' primary distribution channels.

These retailers have physical locations where customers can browse and purchase books in person. Building relationships with bookstores and securing shelf space for publications necessitates an active approach, negotiation, and collaboration with store owners and managers.

To encourage bookshops to carry and promote their books, publishers may offer incentives such as promotional pricing, co-op advertising, and author events. Publishers can also contact online merchants, which include e-commerce sites such as Amazon, Barnes & Noble, and small online bookstores. Online merchants provide readers with the convenience and accessibility of ordering books from the comfort of their own homes and having them delivered directly to their door.

Publishers may increase their exposure on online retail platforms by creating appealing product listings, optimizing keywords and metadata for discoverability, and taking advantage of promotional opportunities such as Amazon's Kindle Direct Publishing Select program. Furthermore, libraries are an essential distribution channel for publishers, providing access to publications for readers who do not have the funds to buy books.

Publishers can provide their products to libraries through library wholesalers and distributors, as well as directly to librarians and library acquisition departments. Participating in library distribution schemes, such as Over Drive's digital lending platform or library consortiums, can increase the exposure and availability of publications to library patrons.

In addition to traditional distribution techniques, digital distribution channels are becoming increasingly important for reaching readers in the digital age. E-book retailers such as the Kindle, Apple Books, and Google Play Books allow publishers to distribute digital versions of their works to an international audience of e-book readers.

Audiobook services such as Audible, Scribd, and Audiobooks.com enable publishers to distribute audiobook copies of their works to listeners who prefer this format. Publishers should consider digital distribution options and utilize online platforms to broaden their reach and accessibility to digitally savvy consumers.

Furthermore, direct-to-consumer sales give publishers another distribution channel for selling publications directly to customers through their own websites or online storefronts. Direct-to-consumer sales provide publishers with greater control over pricing, promotion, and client relationships, as well as higher profit margins than traditional retail channels.

To entice readers to buy straight from the publisher's website, publishers may employ strategies such as special pricing, bundling possibilities, and targeted suggestions. In essence, developing a comprehensive distribution strategy comprises finding and exploiting a variety of distribution channels to effectively reach the target audience.

Publishers can improve the visibility, accessibility, and availability of their publications by developing relationships with traditional bookstores, optimizing their presence on online retail platforms, distributing to libraries, exploring digital distribution options, and implementing direct-to-consumer sales strategies, all of which contribute to the publishing company's success and growth.

Let's go further into the numerous distribution channels and publishing business startup strategies:

1. Brick-and-mortar bookstores: Publishers continue to rely on traditional bookstores for distribution, which provide physical locations for customers to locate and purchase books. Independent bookstores, chain retailers, and specialty stores cater to different demographics and interests, providing publishers with a range of options to contact their clients. Developing relationships with bookstore owners and managers is crucial for obtaining shelf space for publications. Publishers can encourage booksellers to carry and promote their titles by providing incentives such as promotional discounts, author events, and co-op advertising.

2. Online retailers: Books are distributed online, making them more convenient and accessible to people throughout the world. E-commerce platforms such as Amazon, Barnes & Noble, and local online stores help publishers reach a larger audience and increase sales. Publishers may increase their exposure on online retail platforms by creating compelling product listings, optimizing keywords and metadata for discoverability, and participating in promotional programs such as Amazon's Kindle Direct Publishing Select.

3. Libraries: Libraries make books available to people who cannot purchase them. Publishers can deliver their products to libraries through library wholesalers, distributors, or direct contact with librarians and acquisition departments. Participating in library distribution efforts, such as OverDrive's digital lending platform or library consortiums, can help boost publications' exposure and availability to library users.

4. Digital Distribution Platforms: Publishers may contact individuals in the digital age through e-books and audiobooks. E-book retailers such as Kindle, Apple Books, and Google Play Books allow publishers to distribute digital versions of their works all over the world. Publishers such as Audible, Scribed, and Audiobooks.com can provide audiobook versions to listeners who prefer this format. To attract technologically savvy readers, publishers should investigate digital distribution options and utilize online channels.

5. Direct-to-Consumer Sales: Publishers can sell publications directly to customers through their websites or online storefronts. Direct-to-consumer sales provide publishers with greater control over pricing, marketing, and customer relationships. Publishers that sell directly may communicate with readers, gain valuable consumer data, and promote brand loyalty. To summarize, creating a complete distribution plan entails utilizing a variety of channels, including traditional brick-and-mortar bookstores, internet retailers, libraries, digital distribution platforms, and direct-to-consumer sales. Methods such as exclusive pricing, bundling options, and tailored suggestions may encourage users to buy directly from the publisher's website.

Publishers may maximize the visibility, accessibility, and availability of their publications by carefully engaging numerous channels and implementing targeted marketing and promotional efforts, thus contributing to the publishing company's success and development.

Selling and sales strategy

Selling and sales strategy are crucial when starting a publishing company since they include selling publications to specified audiences and driving sales to fulfill revenue objectives. To develop an effective marketing and sales strategy, you must first study your target demographic, then identify promotional channels and tactics for attracting readers and consumers.

The first step in creating a marketing and sales strategy is identifying the target audience for publications. This involves doing market research to gain a deeper understanding of potential readers' demographics, preferences, and behaviors.

When crafting marketing messages and promotional activities for their target audience, publishers should take into account age, gender, interests, reading habits, and purchasing behavior. After determining the target audience, publishers may develop a comprehensive marketing plan that includes a number of promotional tactics for reaching potential readers. Traditional marketing tactics for attracting elder demographics or specialist markets include print advertising, radio commercials, and direct mail. Digital marketing tools such as social media, email marketing, content marketing, and search engine optimization (SEO) are essential for reaching younger demographics and tech-savvy readers. Publishers should employ both online and offline marketing channels to boost reach and engagement with their target audience.

Content marketing is a successful method for publishers to attract and engage readers by providing fascinating and relevant content based on their interests and choices. Publishers can use blog posts, articles, videos, podcasts, and other media to promote their books, authors, and expertise in specific genres or subjects. Content marketing increases brand awareness, authority, and reader connections, ultimately driving traffic to the publisher's website and increasing publication sales.

In addition to content marketing, social media marketing plays a vital role in a publisher's entire marketing and sales strategy. Social media platforms, including Facebook, Instagram, Twitter, LinkedIn, and TikTok, enable publishers to communicate with readers, promote publications, and enhance engagement.

Publishers may generate interest and passion for their publications by publishing excerpts, reviews, author interviews, behind-the-scenes details, and other exciting items. Social media advertising may also help publishers target certain audiences and boost traffic to their websites or online bookstores.

Email marketing is another efficient approach for publishers to connect with their readers and customers, build connections, and boost income. Publishers may utilize customized email campaigns to promote new releases, special offers, author events, and other news to their subscribers. Personalized and segmented email marketing based on reader interests and behavior may enhance engagement and conversion rates, resulting in more sales and money for the publishing company.

Collaboration with book bloggers, influencers, bookstagrammers, and other literary influencers may also help a publisher's marketing efforts reach and impact a larger audience.

Influencers may promote publications to their following through reviews, recommendations, freebies, and sponsored posts, raising visibility and enthusiasm for new releases.

Finally, publishers should implement effective sales strategies to enhance book sales via a number of channels, including direct-to-consumer sales on their website, online retailers, physical bookstores, libraries, and other distribution channels.

Pricing strategy, discount promotions, sales incentives, and relationship building with retailers and wholesalers are all part of optimizing sales opportunities and revenue.

The Significance of Brand Identity

Creating a strong brand identity is essential for establishing a presence in the publishing sector and drawing readers to publications. A well-defined brand identity incorporates elements such as the publisher's logo, website design, typography, color palette, and tone of voice in marketing materials. Consistent branding across all marketing channels and promotional materials helps to create a coherent and recognized brand that interacts with readers while also building trust and confidence.

Another key component of the marketing and sales strategy is the capacity to interact with the literary community and attend relevant events and activities. Attending book fairs, literary festivals, author signings, and other industry events helps you connect with writers, readers, bookshop owners, librarians, and other publishing stakeholders.

Collaborations with literary influencers and thought leaders may help publications increase exposure, reputation, and word-of-mouth referrals.

Furthermore, using data and analytics is crucial for evaluating the success of marketing and sales activities, as well as modifying methods to get better outcomes. Publishers may learn about reader behavior and preferences by measuring metrics such as website traffic, social media engagement, email open rates, click-through rates, conversion rates, and sales performance.

Analyzing data allows publishers to identify patterns, evaluate marketing campaign performance, and make data-driven decisions to improve targeting, messaging, and ROI.

Building a community of loyal readers and followers is essential for long-term success in the publishing industry. Author events, book clubs, online forums, social media groups, and newsletters are some of the ways that publishers may communicate with their fans. Making relationships with readers includes listening to their feedback, responding to their questions and comments, and allowing for involvement and debate. By cultivating a loyal fan base, publishers may build buzz, encourage word-of-mouth referrals, and increase repeat purchases, all of which contribute to long-term growth and success.

Marketing Plan

Creating a marketing plan is a key step in launching a publishing company since it outlines the tactics and procedures for promoting publications to the intended audience and accomplishing marketing objectives.

A comprehensive marketing plan must include a number of important components to ensure its effectiveness and success. To begin, conducting market research is essential for knowing your target audience, identifying industry trends, and evaluating rivals.

Market research includes analyzing demographic data, reader preferences, purchasing behavior, and industry trends to identify possibilities and challenges. Publishers should research the sorts of books that customers prefer, where they buy books, and how they consume book-related media and information. Second, having clearly stated marketing objectives is essential for implementing the marketing strategy and tracking results.

Marketing goals should be SMART (specific, measurable, achievable, relevant, and time-bound). A publishing company's marketing goals may include increasing brand awareness, broadening market reach, driving website traffic, generating leads, increasing book sales, or successfully launching a new publication.

Identifying the target audience is crucial for developing marketing messages and strategies that will be effective with the intended readers. The target audience's demographics may include age, gender, and region, interests, reading habits, and purchasing behavior. Publishers should create buyer personas or profiles of the ideal readers for their publications, taking into account their preferences, needs, and pain points.

A positioning strategy comprises determining the publishing company's unique value proposition and market position for its publications. Publishers should discover the key differentiators that set their publications apart from competitors and effectively communicate these unique selling points to their target audience.

This might involve promoting the material's quality, the writers' expertise, the subjects' relevance, or the publishing brand's originality. Choosing the right marketing channels is essential for reaching your target audience and enhancing the effectiveness of your marketing efforts.

Publishers should experiment with a variety of online and offline marketing channels based on their target audience's preferences and behaviors. Online marketing channels may include social media, email marketing, content marketing, search engine optimization (SEO), online advertising, and influencer partnerships. Offline marketing strategies include print advertising, direct mail, book signings, author events, and attendance at book fairs and literary festivals.

Crafting appealing marketing messaging includes creating content and language that resonates with the target audience and motivates them to take action. Publishers should develop messaging that highlights their publications' unique benefits and features, fulfills the target audience's needs and interests, and effectively communicates the value proposition.

This may contain anecdotes, testimonials, reviews, suggestions, and persuasive language that appeals to readers' emotions and desires. Implementing a content marketing strategy requires creating and distributing valuable, relevant, and engaging information in order to attract and retain the target audience.

Content marketing may take various forms, including blog posts, articles, videos, podcasts, infographics, social media posts, and email newsletters. Publishers should develop a content calendar and schedule content development and distribution to align marketing objectives with the needs and interests of their target audience. Setting a budget and allocating resources are crucial for successfully carrying out the marketing strategy and reaching marketing objectives. Publishers should set a marketing budget and allocate it to various marketing channels, tactics, and campaigns. This might involve investing in paid advertising, hiring marketing experts or firms, outsourcing content generation, or purchasing marketing tools and software.

Finally, evaluating and measuring the efficacy of marketing activities is essential for fine-tuning techniques, enhancing ROI, and reaching marketing objectives. Publishers should keep track of key performance indicators (KPIs) such as website traffic, social media engagement, email open rates, click-through rates, conversion rates, lead generation, book sales, and ROI.

Analyzing data and metrics allows publishers to identify patterns, assess the effectiveness of marketing campaigns, and make data-driven decisions to improve marketing strategies and achieve marketing objectives. In essence creating a marketing plan entails conducting market research, defining marketing objectives, identifying the target audience, developing a positioning strategy, choosing marketing channels, crafting compelling marketing messages, implementing a content marketing strategy, setting a budget and allocating resources, and measuring and evaluating performance.

Publishers may successfully promote their books, attract readers, drive sales, and meet marketing objectives by developing and implementing a comprehensive marketing strategy, therefore contributing to the publishing company's success and growth.

Online Presence

In today's digital age, having an online presence is essential for starting a publishing business. An effective online presence enables publishers to reach a larger audience, market their books, engage readers, and boost income.

Here are some fundamental tips for establishing an online presence:

1. Website Development: Building a professional and user-friendly website is essential for building an online presence. The website serves as the publishing company's primary hub, where readers can learn about publications, authors, upcoming releases, events, and other relevant information. Publishers should invest in developing a visually appealing website that includes easy navigation, book listings, author profiles, and buying options. Optimizing the website for mobile devices and search engines will increase visibility and exposure.

2. Material Creation: To attract and retain visitors to their websites, publishers should produce high-quality, entertaining content. Content production includes blog entries, articles, author interviews, book reviews, excerpts, and multimedia such as films and podcasts. By providing instructional and entertaining information about their books and the publishing industry, publishers may establish themselves as experts in their subject and attract visitors to their website.

3. Establishing a presence on social media is critical for engaging readers, establishing brand awareness, and driving traffic to the publisher's website. Publishers should identify the social media platforms where their target audience is most active and set up profiles on sites such as Facebook, Instagram, Twitter, LinkedIn, and Pinterest. Regularly offering intriguing material, connecting with followers, and participating in book and publishing-related conversations may all help a publisher create a loyal following and expand its online presence.

4. Email Marketing: Email marketing is an effective way to communicate with readers and promote publications. Publishers should compile an email list of subscribers who have consented to receive updates, newsletters, and promotional offers. Sending out frequent emails with updates on new titles, author events, special promotions, and exclusive content may help publishers engage with subscribers and increase traffic to their websites.

5. Online advertising may increase visibility and reach a wider audience. Publishers may target certain demographics, interests, and behaviors using a range of online advertising channels, such as Google AdWords, social media ads, display ads, and sponsored content. Strategic targeting and visually appealing ad creatives may drive traffic to a publisher's website, promote publications, generate leads, and boost sales.

6. Search Engine Optimization (SEO): Making a publisher's website search engine-friendly is critical for improving visibility and ranking in SERPs. Publishers should do keyword research to identify essential keywords for their articles and include them strategically in website content, metadata, and URLs. Optimizing website structure, enhancing page load speed, and obtaining backlinks from reputable websites may all help improve search engine rankings and organic traffic.

7. List your publications on online retail platforms like Amazon, Barnes & Noble, and independent bookshops to reach a larger audience and enhance sales. Publishers may improve product listings by including compelling book descriptions, high-quality cover photographs, and relevant keywords to maximize discoverability and attract new readers.

Monitoring sales performance, customer comments, and competitor activity on online retail platforms may assist publishers in fine-tuning their marketing strategies and optimizing book listings for better visibility and sales. To summarize, establishing an online presence is essential for starting a publishing company and efficiently advertising publications in today's digital environment.

Publishers can build a strong online presence, reach a larger audience, and drive sales and growth for their publishing company by developing a professional website, creating valuable content, establishing a social media presence, implementing email marketing, investing in online advertising, optimizing for search engines, and leveraging online retail platforms.

Sales channels and revenue generation

Sales channels and revenue generation are critical components of starting a publishing company because they determine how publications are sold to customers and how money is generated to sustain the business. Establishing effective sales channels and implementing revenue-generating strategies are important to the publishing company's success and growth. Direct-to-consumer sales are an important sales channel for publishers, allowing them to offer publications directly to customers via their website or online store.

Direct-to-consumer sales provide publishers with greater control over pricing, marketing, and customer relationships. Publishers that sell directly may enhance profits by lowering distributor and retail costs while also creating direct relationships with customers. Implementing tactics such as special pricing, bundling options, and targeted suggestions may entice users to purchase directly from the publisher's website.

Publishers can also sell to online merchants, such as Amazon, Barnes & Noble, and tiny online bookstores. Online retailers assist publishers in reaching a broader audience and increasing earnings by offering their publications on key online platforms.

To improve discoverability and attract purchasers, publishers should enhance product listings with engaging book descriptions, high-quality cover pictures, and relevant keywords. Monitoring sales performance, customer comments, and competitor activity on online retail platforms may assist publishers in fine-tuning their marketing strategies and optimizing book listings for better visibility and sales.

Brick-and-mortar bookstores are another important sales channel for publishers, as they provide real spaces where buyers may browse and purchase books in person. Building relationships with bookstores and securing shelf space for publications necessitates an active approach, negotiation, and collaboration with store owners and managers.

To encourage booksellers to stock and promote their books, publishers could offer incentives such as promotional discounts, co-op advertising, and author events. Libraries also serve as a sales channel for publishers, allowing customers to obtain books that they would not otherwise be able to purchase. Publishers can deliver their products to libraries through library wholesalers, distributors, or direct contact with librarians and acquisition departments.

Participating in library distribution initiatives, such as OverDrive's digital lending platform or library consortiums, can help boost the visibility and availability of publications for library users. In addition to traditional sales channels, publishers may consider other revenue streams to enhance their income.

Licensing and subsidiary rights may include the sale of worldwide rights, translation rights, film and television rights, or audio rights for publications. Publishers can diversify their revenue streams and capitalize on market opportunities by providing ancillary products and services related to their publications, such as merchandise, digital products, instructional courses, and subscription services.

Furthermore, implementing effective pricing strategies is essential for growing revenue and profitability. When determining publication prices, publishers should consider production costs, market demand, competitive pricing, and perceived value. To cater to distinct customer segments, publishers use a pricing approach known as differential pricing, which involves offering numerous editions or formats of a publication at varying prices. Publishers may also employ dynamic pricing systems, which adjust rates based on demand, seasonality, and consumer behavior in order to optimize sales and profits.

Collaboration with writers and influencers

Collaboration with writers and influencers is a vital aspect of starting a publishing company since it may help expand the reach, exposure, and success of publications. Establishing positive relationships with writers and influencers enables publishers to leverage their knowledge, readership, and networks to successfully promote books and increase sales.

Here's an in-depth look at dealing with writers and influencers:

Publishers rely largely on authors to generate the material that drives their libraries. Establishing collaborative partnerships with writers includes fostering open communication, mutual respect, and shared goals in order to succeed together.

Publishers should prioritize building strong relationships with writers based on trust, transparency, and continued support throughout the publishing process.

Collaborating with writers starts with acquiring manuscripts and establishing publishing contracts that outline the terms and conditions of publication, such as royalties, rights, and obligations. To ensure the success of their publications' production and promotion, publishers should work closely with writers, providing editing, design, and marketing aid.

Collaborating on marketing and promotional activities such as book signings, author events, media interviews, and social media campaigns helps to promote the author's work and boost sales. Collaboration with literary and industry experts may help improve publishing success by enhancing reach, validity, and buzz among followers. Influencers include book bloggers, bookstagrammers, booktubers, literary critics, educators, and others who have a significant online presence and impact on the book business.

Collaborating with influencers means looking for partners that share the publisher's brand values, target audience, and genre preferences. Developing connections with influencers begins with targeted outreach, genuine interactions, and common interests. Publishers should hunt for and approach influencers whose content complements their publications and adds value to their audience. Influencer collaborations might include book reviews, author interviews, book features, guest posts, giveaways, and compensated content.

Publishers may encourage influencers to share their honest opinions and ideas with their followers by offering them advance review copies (ARCs) or complimentary copies of books. Building long-term partnerships with authors and influencers requires ongoing communication, collaboration, and support.

Publishers should respond to author and influencer feedback by listening to criticisms, resolving difficulties, and changing their approach. By fostering these collaborative partnerships, publishers may use writers' and influencers' creativity, knowledge, and influence to boost publication visibility and success, ultimately driving sales and growth for the publishing company.

Conclusion

To summarize, starting a publishing company is a complex process that requires careful planning, sound decision-making, and a strong dedication to success. Throughout this thorough book, we have addressed a wide range of crucial elements and problems associated with starting and running a successful publishing company.

We began by discussing the significance of publishing companies in the literary world and how they bring many viewpoints and stories to people all across the world. Understanding the significance of publishing businesses prepares aspiring publishers to embark on their path with a clear sense of purpose and vision.

Next, we addressed the goals of the book "How to Start a Publishing Company," which is a comprehensive guide for anybody interested in entering the publishing industry. The book aims to provide potential publishers with realistic ideas, strategies, and tangible techniques for successfully starting and managing a publishing company.

We then looked into the book's target audience, which includes aspiring publishers, writers, entrepreneurs, industry professionals, and anybody interested in learning about the complexity of the publishing business. Understanding the target audience enables the book to effectively address their needs, challenges, and aspirations in the publishing sector. The publishing entrepreneurship preparation process includes self-assessment, skill appraisal, market research, and firm planning.

To succeed in today's competitive publishing landscape, prospective publishers must possess a blend of creativity, business savvy, industry knowledge, and entrepreneurial energy. Starting a publishing company requires careful consideration of legal and financial problems such as business registration, copyright laws, tax obligations, and financial planning. By addressing these concerns early on, publishers may ensure regulatory compliance while also setting the groundwork for the company's financial health and longevity.

Furthermore, creating a comprehensive marketing plan is essential for promoting publications, attracting readers, and growing income. Publishers may create a strong online presence, connect with their target audience, and build brand awareness by leveraging a number of marketing channels, content development techniques, and promotional strategies. Sales channels and income-generating strategies are crucial for increasing sales and sustaining the publishing firm. Publishers may maximize sales potential and long-term profitability by experimenting with new sales channels, collaborating with authors and influencers, and applying smart pricing and distribution strategies.

To summarize, starting a publishing company requires a combination of passion, creativity, business acumen, and determination. By understanding the key components and issues involved in establishing and operating a publishing company, prospective publishers may confidently embark on their journey and position themselves for success in the dynamic and ever-changing publishing industry.